Where Perseverance Finds Her Voice.

Real Women. Real Stories. Real Transformation.

Empowered Women United Anthology

Volume 1

Compiled by

LaTonya M. Whitehead

I Got Issues™ Publishing

I Got Issues™ Publishing

Featuring Stories by

Kayana Lang

E.N. McMillan

Debra S. Parker

Ashley Titus

Dr. Rachel A. Watkins

Chela Whitehead

Published by

I Got Issues Publishing

Charlotte, North Carolina

ISBN: (979-8-9955024-0-1)

Printed in the United States of America

Dedication

This book is dedicated to every woman who has ever felt broken, overlooked, or silenced.

May these stories remind you that your voice matters, your story matters, and perseverance will always find its way to speak.

Contents

Introduction

LaTonya M. Whitehead

Welcome to ***Where Perseverance Finds Her Voice, Volume 1, an Empowered Women United Anthology.***

Before you read a single chapter, you need to understand what you're holding. This is not just a collection of stories; it's the beginning of a movement. Empowered Women United (EWU) was created for women who are tired of pretending they're okay. Women who love God, love people, and still carry silent battles that don't match their smiles. Women who have survived things they don't even talk about anymore because life forced them to keep moving. Women who have been strong for everybody else, but somewhere along the way forgot what it feels like to be held themselves. EWU exists because too many women are doing life like this: bleeding quietly while serving loudly, showing up polished while breaking down privately, carrying guilt for what happened to them, and shame for how they coped, feeling called, but also feeling stuck, knowing God has more, but not knowing how to get from pieces to purpose.

Therefore, EWU was created to be a space where women can do three things without fear: heal, grow, and rebuild together. Not in a way that's fake. Not in a way that's surface. Not in a way that just shouts, "you got this!" and sends you back into the same patterns, but EWU is a sisterhood with structure. A safe place with standards. A community where your story isn't used against you-it's redeemed. Where you don't have to be perfect to belong, but you do have to be willing to become.

WHY IS THIS BOOK CALLED VOLUME 1?

We call this book Volume 1 because this is what EWU represents: a starting point. For some women, EWU is the beginning of telling the truth without feeling condemned. For others, it's the beginning of forgiving without returning to what broke them. For others, it's the beginning of setting boundaries without guilt. For others, it's the beginning of rebuilding confidence after betrayal, divorce, addiction, abuse, grief, rejection, or failure. And for many, it's the beginning of finding purpose after years of surviving.

This isn't the end of the story. Because the truth is: the issue may have introduced itself loudly, but it does not get to write the last chapter.

WHY WE CREATED THIS ANTHOLOGY SERIES

This anthology series was created because we kept seeing the same thing: Women weren't lacking talent. Women weren't lacking faith. Women were lacking permission to be honest about the process. Some women don't need another cute quote. They need proof. Proof that you can lose yourself and still find your way back. Proof that you can make a mistake and still be called. Proof that you can be embarrassed, exposed, delayed, disappointed, and still rise. That's why these stories matter. Because when one woman finds her voice, she gives another woman language for what she's been living through. And once you finally have language, you can finally start healing.

WHAT DOES "ISSUE TO SUCCESS" MEAN IN THIS BOOK?

When we say issue to success, we are not talking about a perfectly edited life. We're talking about the kind of success people can't always clap for because it doesn't always look flashy, but it is holy. Success is when you stop apologizing for surviving, you stop shrinking to make others comfortable, you stop calling your healing "extra," you stop wearing strength as a mask, and start building it as a lifestyle.

In success, you learn how to stand again, but this time with wisdom, boundaries, and a backbone. Success is when your story stops being a wound you hide and becomes a light you carry.

And I need you to catch this: perseverance is not denial. Perseverance is not pretending it didn't hurt. Perseverance is not smiling through what's killing you. Perseverance is telling the truth and still choosing to move forward. It's crying, praying, getting help, setting the boundary, making the decision, and taking the next step, even when your voice shakes. That's why we say: Where perseverance finds her voice. Because perseverance will introduce you to parts of you that comfort could never.

A NOTE TO THE WOMAN WHO FEELS BEHIND

If you're reading this and you feel behind in life, hear me clearly: You are not behind. You are becoming. Some things took longer because they were being built deeper.
Some seasons felt silent because God was strengthening your roots. Some delays were protective. Some endings were rescue. Some losses were redirection. You are allowed to start again.

You are allowed to heal without explaining yourself to people who never carried your pain.

You are allowed to rebuild without begging for permission. And if nobody has told you lately, the fact that you're still here is evidence that your story isn't finished.

HOW TO READ THIS BOOK

I want you to do three things as you read:

1. Listen for the part that sounds like you.
    There will be a sentence, a moment, a confession, a turning point that feels familiar. That's not a coincidence. That's the connection.

2. Honor the courage it takes to tell the truth. Telling your story is not just writing words; it's reopening rooms you worked so hard to close. But healing has a way of turning keys into freedom.

3. Decide that your story isn't over.
    Let these pages be proof that God can redeem what life tried to ruin and that your "issue" can become an assignment.

If you're the type who likes something practical, here are three questions to ask yourself after each chapter:

What part of this story challenged me? What part of this story felt like me? What is one step I need to take next?

THIS IS SISTERHOOD WITH SUBSTANCE

Empowered Women United is not a cute name. It's a declaration. United means we don't compete; we cover. United means we tell the truth and still choose love. United means we don't weaponize our sister's past; we witness her comeback.
United means we stop acting like we have to suffer

alone to prove we're strong.

Strength isn't isolation. Strength is learning how to heal in community without losing yourself. So, if you've been carrying your story like a secret, I want you to know, you are safe here.

Before you turn the page.

I want you to make one decision right now: Don't just read this book; receive it. Let it challenge you. Let it correct you. Let it comfort you. Let it call you higher. And when you finish, I want you to be able to say: "My story didn't stop at the issue. I found my voice."

Welcome to your voice.
-LaTonya M. Whitehead
Empowered Women United

CHAPTER 1: THROUGH THE FIRE

Kayana Lang

After nine months in Little Rock, Arkansas, with my daughter while she waited for and received a heart transplant, coming home felt like we could finally breathe again. I was excited, relieved, and grateful. We moved into a four-bedroom, two-bath trailer that felt perfect for our family. It wasn't fancy, but it was ours, a fresh start.

But after we settled in, I started noticing small issues: outlets that didn't work and lights that flickered, especially when the microwave was on. I reported the problems to the landlord. Some things got fixed, but others were left untouched.

After a while, I stopped expecting a response. I'd report something, then just let it go, because nothing ever changed. Still, I kept hearing this quiet nudge in my spirit: "Tell the landlord one more time, tell him one more time." Of course, I ignored it, not because I didn't hear it, but because I didn't believe it would matter. I didn't realize that voice wasn't pushing me to complain. It was trying to protect me.

The kids were adjusted to school and daycare, and I was ready to get back into the workforce. I was extremely nervous that morning—standing there overthinking what to wear, like it was going to decide my whole future.. In the midst of getting ready, I heard that same soft but stern voice again: "Wear the pantsuit." Like a kid pouting, I didn't want to. It felt too plain. I wanted to wear my skirt set instead.

As I pulled the skirt out and tried to put it on, I realized the button was gone. I searched for a safety pin or anything, because I was determined to make it work. So, with no other choice, I put on the pantsuit.

When I arrived at the interview, I couldn't believe it, and the interviewer and I were wearing the same suit, just in different colors. It instantly broke the tension.

We laughed, the conversation flowed, and the interview went great. That moment should've taught me something: when that voice speaks, it's not random; it's protection. But I still didn't realize how serious it was, at least, not yet. I got the job, but more than that, I got another reminder: when that voice speaks, it's never just about the moment. It's always about what's coming. The real lesson wasn't the job; the real lesson was the voice.

Every Sunday, I prepared for the week by washing, ironing, and laying out the kids' clothes so everything would be easy to grab and go. It was a system we had followed for years, and it worked. But as the day went on, I kept hearing that voice again. You know the same voice I had been ignoring, the one I kept brushing off as me being an overthinker. This time it said: "Put the kids' uniforms, birth certificates, Social Security cards, your driver's license, and important documents in a tote by the front door." I paused. Because who does that? I remember thinking, *" That makes no sense. "* Then I said it out loud to myself: "What sense does that make? I'm not doing that." And I went right on with my day.

A few hours later, I was in the kitchen cooking dinner, and there it was again. That voice. But this time it wasn't gentle. It was louder. Urgent. Like it didn't have time to keep asking.

"Put the kids' uniforms, birth certificates, Social Security cards, your driver's license, and your important documents in a tote by the front door." I stopped what I was doing and looked around because of the way it hit me, I just knew somebody else had to hear it too.

My heart started racing. My stomach tightened. And then my mind kicked in, fighting it. *Why would I do that? Who packs documents for no reason? Nothing is happening. I'm just being dramatic.* So, I did what I had gotten good at doing. I swallowed it. I shook it off. I turned back to the stove… and kept cooking. The whole time I was stirring pots, God was trying to prepare me for what I didn't see coming.

Later that night, while I was getting the kids ready for bed, that voice came again, only this time it was louder. So loud that I asked my oldest two, "Did y'all hear that?" They looked at me and said, "No ma'am, we didn't hear anything." That's when it hit me: *Am I losing it?*

Once everyone was finally in bed and asleep, I poured myself a glass of red wine, grabbed the book I'd been reading, and got comfortable. After a couple of chapters, as I was sipping and reading, there it was again: "Put the important things in a tote by the front door.

At this point, I honestly assumed it was just me hearing things. So, I ignored it and kept reading until my eyes got heavy. I closed the book, took one last sip, prayed a simple prayer, and started drifting off.

But maybe five minutes later, that voice came again so loud it startled me. It scared me so bad it felt like somebody was standing right beside my bed. I jumped up, turned on the light, and didn't see anything. I walked through the house, checked the rooms, checked the doors— nothing. Nobody. Just my family, asleep. I climbed back into bed, shaken and nervous, and tried to convince myself to go to sleep.

All of a sudden, I snapped awake again—only this time, the voice sounded like my mother. And that's what scared me the most. It had been over twenty years since I'd heard my mother's voice. She passed when I was young, but I would recognize her anywhere. I knew it couldn't really be her… but it was that same stern tone; the one that used to stop me in my tracks. In that moment, I didn't feel confused anymore. I felt warned. I knew if I didn't move, something was about to happen.

So yes, I jumped my tail out of that bed. I left one uniform out for each child and put the rest in the tote, along with our important documents.

The whole time I was moving, I felt crazy, but something in me kept saying, "Trust. Have faith." There I was, closing the tote, sliding it right by the front door, and trying to calm my hands down.

The next morning felt normal. I was dressing the kids, combing hair, reminding them to brush their teeth—doing what moms do. Then out of nowhere, my oldest ran in and shouted, "Mama... my brother's room is on fire!" I jumped up and ran to the room, and oh my Lord, it really was. Flames were already climbing, and within seconds, it was spreading fast. I didn't even think. I just moved. I was only wearing a tank top and shorts, but like any mama bear, I only thought of protecting my cubs. So, I grabbed my babies and ran out of the trailer into the drizzling rain, standing at the curb in shock, watching our home turn into chaos. Volunteer firefighters arrived first within minutes, and the fire department pulled up shortly after, but those minutes felt like days as the blaze grew. And all I could think was: We're losing everything on my first day back to work. Losing everything on my first day of starting over.

Standing there in despair, one of the firefighters placed his hand on my shoulder and asked if I could move my car because it was parked too close to the trailer. The thought of the flames reaching my car scared me even more.

That's when it hit me. I slapped my forehead and called myself a dummy because my keys were still inside, left on my nightstand beside the bed. This was the moment my "new beginning" became real... and heartbreaking.

Through tears, my daughter tried to run back inside to save her fish, and I had to stop her. I stood there watching the flames swallow our home, our furniture, pictures, and memories, thinking about my first day back to work, shattered before it even started. Even now, writing this and remembering that day, I don't think I've ever prayed as hard as I prayed in those moments.

Finally, the fire was out, and all that was left was the shell of what had once been our double-wide trailer, our home. When I walked up to what was left of the front door frame, everything was black, wet, and melted. I stepped inside and did a quick walk-through, hoping there might be something, anything, to save. But there were no pictures. No toys. Nothing left untouched. Our "new beginning" started with nothing.

Later, the fire chief met me outside and said, "This fire started because of the faulty wiring, but there was one thing that survived completely untouched." He pointed and said, "That green tote by the door." I froze. Shock hit me first, then relief, then gratitude, then tears. I fell to my knees right there, praising God, thanking Him for loving me enough to make me listen. Because now I understood: God wasn't trying to control me. He was trying to cover me. That day taught me to slow down long enough to hear Him.

To stop calling conviction "overthinking." To stop brushing off instructions just because they don't make sense in the moment. And here's what I know now: I lost a home… but I didn't lose what mattered most. The fire took what was replaceable, but God protected what was necessary. And that's how I know He will walk with you through the fire, too. Sometimes God won't shout to scare you; He will speak to save you. So, if He tells you, "One more time," listen.

About The Author

Kayana Lang

Kayana Lang is a devoted mother of four and a nurse passionate about promoting safe sexual practices and education. She is the owner of Yana's Beauty Treats, a business inspired by her personal journey with eczema. Through her story, Kayana encourages healing, growth, and connection as sisters in Christ.

CHAPTER 2: ALREADY HER

E. N. McMillan

The last time we talked, we discussed preparing to be selfish in a healthy way. We talked about the importance of setting

boundaries, stopping people-pleasing, ditching procrastination, leaving fear behind, and choosing to love yourself. Now that we've addressed those things, what's next?

Let's briefly revisit why each one matters and how we move forward from here, because when you set healthy boundaries, remember: no one is off-limits. Boundaries should include everyone who has access to you. No one should have more access to you than God, and even you. I know that may be difficult for some to hear.

But let's be honest. If you are constantly making time for others and doing all the things for everyone else, when do you replenish? When do you recover? When do you restore? Are you operating on fumes or pouring from half a cup?

If you're running on empty, when do you have time for God? When do you have time for yourself? Are you truly showing up as your best self? If you're honest, there's probably a "no" somewhere in there. Many of us have been guilty of putting on a cape, wearing multiple hats, and neglecting our own happiness and purpose. But if you've never taken time to establish healthy boundaries, this is your moment.

You can begin right now. It is never too late. Boundaries protect your time and energy. But there is another habit that quietly erodes both, and that's people-pleasing. So, let's talk about it.

When are you going to stop people-pleasing? I know it's not easy, but it is necessary. Sometimes we don't even realize we're doing it. We say yes when we really mean no. We show up tired. We overcommit. We avoid difficult conversations just to keep the peace. But at what cost? Pressure to perform. Pressure to be liked. Pressure to never disappoint anyone.

And here's the truth: if you are constantly focused on keeping everyone else comfortable, you will eventually become uncomfortable in your own life. Your new way of living requires you to be fully present. Fully aware. Fully honest. You cannot treat your life like a drive-thru, grabbing whatever approval is handed to you just to keep moving. This journey will take time, resilience, patience, and faith. And you cannot fully show up if you are constantly trying to please other people.

Take a moment and really think about it. How much time is spent doing things for others out of obligation instead of alignment? How often do you agree to something simply because you don't want to disappoint someone?

Every "yes" that is not aligned with your purpose quietly delays the life you say you want. Time is something we cannot get back. Use it wisely.

We all have a story in this thing called life. And life has not always been kind to many of us; it could have been because of our choices, circumstances, or the actions of others. Nevertheless, we cannot give up.

We can hold ourselves accountable, but we cannot stay stuck there. God forgives all sin. No matter the situation, movement is necessary.

How many times have you said, "I'll do it later"? I know I have, more than once. But I am learning to be intentional and handle things as they come. Do not let procrastination keep you from your purpose or from living the life God has called you to live.

The adversary is strategic. He will steal your time, waste your time, and trap you in regret. If your relationship with God is not strong, you may find yourself constantly living in "what I should have done." You'll stay on a merry-go-round, going in circles with no plan, no dreams, no clear purpose, and no intention of getting off. Always remember who you belong to. And always remember that each of us has a purpose for our lives.

I know this may be a lot to process, but I have one more point; stay with me, sis. This is a big one. Leave fear where it is. We are no longer giving life to fear. We are no longer overthinking every move. I am not saying do not plan or be wise. I am saying we cannot continue allowing fear to dictate our lives. Fear has a way of whispering worst-case scenarios and magnifying every possible failure. If we are not careful, it will slowly convince us that staying safe is better than stepping forward, and there is someone right now so fearful that things will go wrong, they cannot even imagine them going right.

Fear has narrowed their vision. It has convinced them that struggle is permanent and that better is not possible. But what if fear is not the truth? What if it is simply a barrier? What if God is waiting on you to shift your mindset, to believe that more is available? What if He is waiting on your surrender, not your perfection? Sometimes, the very thing standing between us and a life of abundance, joy, love, and peace is not circumstance; it's agreement with fear. So, what would your "yes" look like? Because somewhere along the way, many of us stopped dreaming. When did it happen for you? And what would happen if you chose to dream again? The beautiful part is that you would not be doing it alone. God loves us. His love is patient, faithful, gracious, and merciful. He does not call us forward without also equipping us.

He gives us what we need, including the courage to believe and the capacity to grow, and I had that truth in one of the hardest seasons in my life.

About six years ago, life had me in a chokehold. I mean, I was definitely on a merry-go-round and did not know how to get off. I have always maintained employment to take care of myself. But being a single mother made life especially challenging. I decided to go back to school to pursue a master's degree in clinical Mental Health Counseling. At the time, it felt like the right thing to do.

I am not someone who quits, but I was close to the edge. I was physically exhausted.

Mentally drained. Financially overwhelmed. I was working full-time, parenting full-time, attending class, and trying to complete an internship. I cried many nights. I was overwhelmed and tired, but I demanded a different life.

I didn't know when it would happen, but I believed God would move. He had promised me some things, and a different life was one of them. I knew my hard work was not in vain, but relief felt so far away.

Yes, I can step to the front of the line. I was her, living paycheck to paycheck, robbing Peter to pay Paul and everybody else. I was barely paying my mortgage on time. It was tough. My back was against the wall.

But I knew God's Word was true. I just had to figure out what He wanted me to do. God needed me to finish my internship and graduate in 2019 because little did we know, the world was about to shut down.

In October 2019, I proudly graduated with my master's degree in clinical Mental Health Counseling. I had already started searching for better employment. I found a position on Indeed that caught my interest. I applied. I interviewed.

I received the offer. I had no idea that all I needed to do was finish. By November 2019, I was working at my new job, making more money. I could finally breathe. God placed me in a position where I could no longer let fear, procrastination, people-pleasing, or lack of boundaries lead my life. I had to do something different.

God kept me. God pushed me. And when I gave God my "yes," doors began to open. Within two months, I was working from home because of COVID-19. I no longer had to pay for after-school care for my son. Look at God! And as we continue this journey of life, God creates a new spirit within us. He removes, replaces, and provides what we need to move toward our purpose.

I want to remind someone: you are already her. Whether you leave old mindsets behind, relocate, strengthen your mental capacity, learn a new skill, deepen your relationship with God, or reclaim your power, you were already here. You may not have had everything you needed for the change, but God provides. Your "yes" activates change. It may not come suddenly, but it will come. Things rarely change on our timeline; they change in God's time. Sometimes we forget He is omnipresent. He knows all. He knows when the shift is necessary and when the blessing is needed. And He will lead you toward your purpose.

It is my prayer that this encourages someone to own who they are; to stand bold, confident, and anchored in God as they walk into this new journey. I cannot tell you how or when things will change for you, but I can encourage you to prepare. No matter how difficult it may seem, it will work out. Do not give up on yourself because your life truly depends on it. Every move and every choice you make shapes what happens next. And if you take a wrong step, don't beat yourself up. Get up and keep going.

We have already discussed what the adversary uses to keep us stagnant. And truthfully, he rarely uses anything new. It may come with a different name or face, but it often attacks the same vulnerable places.

Friend, you do not have to do this alone. Find a few people, a community that can walk with you through this journey. Find people who pour into you and whom you can pour into as well. Find those who empower you, challenge you, and hold you accountable.

I look forward to hearing your story. Until then, keep God first. Take it one day at a time. Push through and remember, whatever God has told you to do, do it. He will provide. You are already her.

About The Author

E.N. McMillan

E.N. McMillan is a self-love advocate, devoted mother, and co-author of The Brown Girl Guidebooks: Start with Self Love. She is also the owner of More Than Ragz, an online boutique that inspires confidence and style. Through her work, Ebony empowers women to embrace self-worth and personal growth unapologetically.

A Personal Reflection

Debra S. Parker

There are moments in life when the only way I can truly express my gratitude to God is by remembering who He has been to me. Through every season, both difficult and joyful, I have discovered that God reveals Himself in so many ways. He has been my comfort in hard moments, my strength when I felt weak, my refuge when life felt overwhelming, and my peace when my heart needed reassurance.

As I began reflecting on the faithfulness of God in my life, I realized there are countless ways He has revealed Himself to me. Each name, each attribute, and each role reminds me that I have never walked through life alone. He has been present in every chapter, guiding, protecting, restoring, and reminding me that His love never fails.

The words that follow are my personal reflection of who God has been to me throughout my journey.

Line by line, they represent the many ways I have come to know Him as Savior, protector, provider, healer, and friend.

This poem is more than just words on a page. It is a declaration of faith and gratitude. As you read the poem that follows, my prayer is that you will pause and reflect on the many ways God has shown Himself in your own life as well.

After going through seven surgeries on my leg following an incident while helping a patient, enduring countless therapies, and facing recovery with little to no support, I came face to face with my own limitations- and God's sufficiency. In the moments when I could have given up, He became everything I needed. Today, I am walking again. I am working again as a registered nurse. And more than anything, I am still discovering my purpose in Him- Jesus, my Lord.

CHAPTER 3: YOU ARE™

You are almighty, the author of my faith and my access to abundant life.

You are the beginning and the end, the

bright and morning star, and you are my bread of life.

You are the chief cornerstone, my comforter, my counselor, and my conqueror.

You are my deliverer, my dwelling place, My desire and you are my destiny.

You are excellent, eternal, and you are my essential. You are my father, faith, and my friend.

You are God alone, and you are my grace.

You are my hiding place, my helper, my healer. You are Jehovah, and you are my joy.

You are I Am, and you are my inspiration. You are King of Kings, the keeper of my soul. You are love, the light of the world,

And you are the lifter of my head.

You are the mighty one, my mediator, and you are my master.

You are the name above all names, and you are my novel.

You are omniscient, omnipresent, and omnipotent, and you are my oasis.

You are the Prince of Peace,

my protector, my provider, and you are my praise. You are the quickening spirit, and my quest of life.

You are righteous, my redeemer, my refuge, my restorer, and you are my rock.

You are my savior, my shepherd, my strength, and my song.

You are truth, and you are my trust.

You are unconditional, undeniable, and you are my umbrella of life.

You are victorious, my vindicator, and you are the voice.

You are worthy, you are the Word, and you are wonderful.

You are Yahweh, you are yes and amen,

you are the zeal of my life, and you are my Jesus.

Forever Grateful

Debra S. Parker

About The Author

Debra S. Parker

Debra S. Parker is a mother, grandmother, great-grandmother, and registered nurse.

A survivor of traumatic experiences over three years, she shares her story through poetry as a testament of resilience and healing.

CHAPTER 4: WHEN MOTHERHOOD MADE ME CHOOSE

Ashley Titus

Before I became a mother, I lived in the in- between. Not lost. Not reckless. Not faithless. Just divided. I knew how to pray

fervent prayers, lift my hands in worship, and speak life into other people's situations. But in the quiet places of my own decisions, I hesitated. I negotiated. I delayed. I loved God, but I loved control more. There were rooms in my life I invited Him into, and doors I kept firmly closed. I stood comfortably on a fence built from fear and ambition, certainty and doubt. One foot in surrender.

One foot in self-preservation. From the outside, I was steady. Capable. Responsible. Inside, I was unsettled. Then motherhood arrived, not gently, not passively, but like a divine interruption. And everything I thought I had balanced began to tilt.

Because what I had called balance was really hesitation. I had been living on a fence.

Straddling a fence feels stable until you try to move forward. It is a place of delay disguised as discernment. A place of comfort dressed up as wisdom. You tell yourself you are waiting on God, when in truth, you are waiting on guarantees, and I had mastered the art of partial obedience. I would say yes to the visible things, you know, the safe things. The public expressions of faith. The roles that required strength but not surrender. But when obedience demanded sacrifice, vulnerability, or confrontation, I hesitated.

I postponed healing because productivity felt more impressive. I delayed difficult conversations because peacekeeping felt easier. I silenced conviction because it threatened the life I had curated. And slowly, subtly, I built a life that looked aligned but wasn't anchored.

You can live there for years, in that delicate balance between belief and boldness, until something forces you to choose. For me, that something was her. There is a moment when a child is placed in your arms and time fractures. The room may still be loud. Machines may still hum. Voices may still move around you. But something inside goes quiet. When I first held her, awe and fear braided themselves together in my chest. She was perfect.

I was not. I remember studying her face as if it held a prophecy. As if her existence carried a message I had not yet decoded. And beneath the tenderness was a trembling realization: She would learn strength from watching mine. She would learn faith from observing my surrender. She would learn resilience from witnessing my response to hardship.

Children do not study our words first. They study our consistency. And I knew, in that sacred and terrifying moment, that I could not teach her to fully depend on God while I remained partially dependent on myself. Motherhood did not expose my flaws to shame me. It revealed to them to refine me. And refinement has a way of holding up a mirror. One that reflects what we would rather avoid.

Motherhood is a mirror you cannot turn away from. It reflects your patience and your impatience; your tenderness and your triggers; your faith and your fear. In her presence, I saw generational patterns I had normalized. I saw people-pleasing disguised as kindness. Control disguised as leadership. Fear disguised as caution. I saw how often I dimmed myself to maintain comfort. How frequently I delayed obedience because it threatened familiarity. And I began asking questions that would not leave me alone: What am I modeling? What will she inherit if I refuse to evolve? What cycles will continue because I choose comfort over courage?

It is one thing to tolerate your own stagnation. It is another to realize your child may absorb it, and that awareness unsettled me. And in that holy discomfort, something began to shift.

Transformation is rarely loud. It happens in whispered prayers. In therapy rooms. In boundaries drawn without applause. In tears shed where no one is watching. The fight did not look glamorous. It looked like choosing counseling when silence would have been easier. Confronting insecurities, I had learned to manage instead of healing. Walking away from environments that fed my ego but starved my growth. It looked like obedience when obedience cost me.

There were days I felt stretched between ambition and presence, between building and nurturing, between the woman I had been and the woman I sensed I was becoming.

I often thought about David, not the crowned king, but the flawed man who authored Psalm 51 in the aftermath of failure. His repentance was not polished. It was desperate. It was honest and unhidden. And yet, God did not discard him. That truth anchored me.

Failure, I learned, is not the end of calling. It is often the doorway to deeper surrender. When I hit brick walls, and I did, I stopped interpreting them as rejection. I began seeing them as redirection. When I stumbled, I stopped narrating it as a disqualification. I began to understand that God is less interested in flawless performance and more invested in surrendered hearts, and motherhood intensified that lesson. Because she deserved a mother who rose after falling. And when you realize someone is watching your evolution, delay is no longer harmless; it is generational. And once I understood that, I could no longer stay the same. Awareness demanded action.

There were parts of me that had to die. Excuses that sounded reasonable. Timelines I clung to. Versions of myself that were impressive but incomplete.

Dying to comfort is not poetic. It is painful. It requires saying no when yes would earn applause. It requires choosing growth when stagnation feels familiar. It requires stepping fully off the fence without seeing the full landscape ahead. But I could no longer afford divided living. She was watching. And I wanted her to see a woman who chose alignment over approval.

So, I began saying "no" without apology, "yes" without hesitation, and "not anymore" without guilt. Slowly, the woman who once negotiated her obedience began to embody it.

Becoming is not dramatic. It is disciplined. It is the daily decision to pray when you are tired. To trust when outcomes are uncertain. To lead even while you are still learning.

There was no lightning-bolt moment where I felt fully transformed. Instead, there were hundreds of small, unseen choices that quietly accumulated into strength. I became clearer. Clearer about my voice. Clearer about my purpose. Clearer about the weight and the beauty of legacy. Motherhood did not interrupt my calling. It clarified it. God did not give me her as a distraction from destiny. He gave me her as a direction.

In raising her, I was being raised, refined, stretched, and matured. I did not become perfect. I became aligned. And alignment silences confusion.

And one day, daughter, if you read this, I want you to know something: With God, all things are possible. Not because life will unfold without fracture, but because surrender fortifies you from within. You will experience highs and lows. You will make mistakes. You will hit walls that make you question your strength. Do not interpret those moments as endings. Remember the story of David, who was flawed, repentant, and restored. Remember that falling does not erase calling. Rise again. Give the testimony of how God carried you through what you thought would break you. You were my greatest blessing.

In more ways than you will ever fully understand, you saved my life. You forced clarity where I had been comfortable with confusion. You demanded courage where I had tolerated delay.

You called me forward. It was not always easy. Some seasons were heavy. Some nights were long. Some prayers were whispered through exhaustion. But every stretch strengthened me. You did not simply make me a mother. You made me choose. And in choosing you, I had to confront the woman I had been avoiding.

Straddling the fence once felt strategic. Now I know it was stagnation. Motherhood moved me from hesitation to surrender. It moved me from partial obedience to wholehearted trust, from curated strength to authentic dependence. It did not remove fear. It reduced its authority. It did not eliminate hardship. It infused it with meaning. And if there is one truth I carry now, it is this: God will use what He places in your arms to transform what He has placed in your heart. For me, it was a daughter. For you, it may be something else. But when He calls you forward, do not remain divided. Step fully into the woman you are becoming. Because on the other side of surrender is not perfection. It is a purpose. And purpose will always require your whole yes.

About The Author

Ashley Titus

Ashley Titus is a speaker, mother, and advocate for women discovering strength through life's transitions. Her journey through motherhood and personal transformation reshaped her understanding of faith, obedience, and legacy. Today, she encourages women to rise, rebuild, and become everything God created them to be.

CHAPTER 5: LEADING WHILE LAMENTING: PURPOSED AT A PRICE

Dr. Rachel A. Watkins

My name is Rachel, the youngest of six children, born and raised in Indianapolis, Indiana. I was raised in a two-parent home with Christian values, surrounded by lots of love and encouragement. Over the years, I have collected many titles, including sister, daughter, friend, wife, bonus mom, intercessor, encourager, career woman, travel enthusiast, visionary, and believer. The most challenging title I have held, however, is that of a leader.

Leadership was not something I chose, but I can remember as a little girl always being the one willing to forge her own path, even if I had to go alone. Which reminds me, there is one title I forgot to mention: "preschool dropout." There is a running joke in my family that I am the only child who ever dropped out of preschool. Although it was short-lived, the bigger question is why my parents allowed me to do it.

My parents have always given me the space to try new things and take calculated risks. I am thankful they allowed me to discover exactly who God created me to be and encouraged me to reach for the stars.

You may be wondering why I chose to call this chapter Leading While Lamenting. First, we should start with a definition. The word lament is defined as a passionate expression of grief or sorrow. Webster's Dictionary defines it as expressing sorrow, mourning, or regret, often demonstratively. The Bible has an entire book dedicated to lamenting, and I would encourage you to read it. The Book of Lamentations is a collection of five poetic laments mourning the destruction of Jerusalem, traditionally attributed to the prophet Jeremiah. The book not only validates human sorrow but also affirms God's compassion, offering hope for restoration.

This chapter shares my journey as a leader while lamenting, and how it ultimately led me to purpose.

My story began when I was promoted to Director of Pharmacy at a small rural hospital for the organization I had worked for 13 years. My career path had been full of many twists and turns, but I never anticipated this career leap.

Prior to my promotion, I had grown professionally as a leader and worked my way up from a frontline staff pharmacist all the way to a pharmacy supervisor. In my mind, the next career move would be to a pharmacy manager's role. I heard about an opening for a manager's role, so I applied, but I did not get the position. At that moment, I felt rejected like so many times before, but I decided to persevere.

A few months later, I saw an opening for a director's role, and I decided to apply. The moment I hit submit on my application, I began questioning not only my chances of getting an interview but also my ability to succeed in the role.. I made it to the final round of interviews, and within a few days, I was offered the position. Most people would have been excited, but I had so many mixed emotions, including fear running through my body.

For context, this period of time was in the middle of a pandemic. During COVID, so many people were worried about whether they were going to survive day to day, and here I was adding more responsibilities to my plate. How was I going to lead a team through something the world had never experienced before? So many questions started running through my head: Do I have what it takes to lead an entire department?

Will they like me? What if I make a mistake? Are you crazy? Do you really want to take on a role like this in the middle of a pandemic? What if you can't overcome the learning curve? What if the three-hour round-trip commute becomes too much for you?

Yes, you read that right, three hours round trip. Not only did I have to tackle a learning curve, but I also had to prepare myself mentally for a hefty daily commute. Another concern I had was going into an environment that did not have many people who looked, talked, thought, or had a similar upbringing to mine. I grew up in a big city and spent all of my career in a big city. How was I going to fit into a small rural town that was one hour away from the city?

I had all these questions and more, but then I stumbled upon a quote that gave me the courage to move forward. The quote by Erin Hanson is, "What if I fall? Oh, but my darling, what if you fly?" After reading the quote, it was at that moment I decided to do the job scared, no matter what it took. In the weeks leading up to my first day, I had pep talks with myself about what was happening, and I even had a brunch celebration with some of my girlfriends to keep me motivated.

One thing I've learned about Black women is that we will always support each other in doing challenging things. My support system over the course of my career has been monumental, and I would not be the woman I am today without it.

On my first day of the job, I remember using my commute as an opportunity to pray and seek God. Fear started to creep in, but God reminded me that He was with me. Prayer and the Word of God became tools that carried me through the next four years of challenges. Using my commute to pray became part of my daily routine. I am sure on some days I looked a little crazy praying so fervently in my car, but I never let that stop me. I was determined to be successful in my new role, and I knew God was the only one who could provide a strategy for me.

One scripture that I held tightly to during this season was 2 Corinthians 1:3–4 (NIV): "Praise be to the God and Father of our Lord Jesus Christ, the Father of compassion and the God of all comfort, who comforts us in all our troubles, so that we can comfort those in any trouble with the comfort we ourselves receive from God."

Every ounce of support and comfort God provided to me during that season ultimately allowed me to comfort others.

On my first day at the job, I walked into a department that included no one who looked like me or shared the same upbringing. I was immediately viewed as an outsider because I transferred from a big city hospital to a small rural hospital. The team had been without a leader for at least four months, so I knew I had a challenge on my hands. Not to mention, there was hostility present because two teammates who had applied for the role were now my direct reports. I knew I had to tread lightly, knowing there were people who wanted me to fail and others who were used to doing things their own way. "Jesus, take the wheel," is all I could say, and that is exactly what Jesus did.

Some of the challenges I encountered throughout my journey included supporting my team and patients through COVID, overcoming a steep learning curve, managing operational projects, adjusting workflows, implementing an electronic medical record system, and harmonizing service lines.

While I was caring for my team during COVID, I also had to maintain my own physical, spiritual, and emotional well-being, and some days were really hard. However, the challenges I faced brought me closer to God. I can remember praying daily on my commute to work and asking God to give me wisdom on how to lead this team with all the challenges at hand. As I prayed daily, I felt prepared for the task professionally, but I did not know what was on the horizon in my personal life.

This is where my story shifts to lamenting. As I was navigating leading a new team, I encountered four events in my personal life that caused me to lament. Somewhere along the way, I was taught that leaders never show weakness, and that is something I carried. Although I was about to encounter some of the toughest circumstances I had ever faced, I told myself I still needed to show up for my team no matter what.

The first circumstance I experienced was two failed rounds of IUI (intrauterine insemination) and the infertility issues associated with it. From the day we were married, my husband and I tried desperately to conceive. After trying for eight years, we were losing hope and decided to pursue IUI. Infertility is an incredibly isolating experience. Doctor's appointments with very few answers began to take a toll on me emotionally, spiritually, and physically. God had shown me visions of motherhood, and people had prophesied children over our situation many times, yet our reality did not match what we expected.

I was the only woman in my family with a doctorate degree, but I could not get pregnant. Infertility has a way of making you question yourself as a woman and feel like your body has failed you.

During this time, I also encountered women sharing pregnancy announcements. On some days, that was painful to hear, knowing I might never experience that moment. At the same time, God burdened my heart to pray for other women facing infertility. As I prayed, I saw miracle after miracle happen for them while my own womb remained empty. In that season, I truly learned what intercession looks like. You must pray for what God wants you to pray for, regardless of how much pain you are experiencing.

I prayed for these women's wombs as if they were my own, which required a great sacrifice given what I was facing internally.

I remember the first round of IUI clearly. After taking the necessary medication, I was hopeful. During the procedure, the room felt cold and quiet, and I prayed for a miracle as the insemination took place. Afterward, we went home and began the waiting period. Just as I had done for years, I prayed for a missed period. A few weeks later, I learned that I was not pregnant. In that moment, I felt overwhelming sadness, defeat, and grief. However, I did not have much time to process those emotions because I was leading a healthcare team during a pandemic. Six months later, we tried another round of IUI with the same result. The grief the second time was even heavier. I cried out to God, asking why I had to endure such a painful process. There is a unique weight that comes with grieving something that never fully existed. I felt ashamed for grieving a baby that was never conceived, but in reality, I was mourning the loss of my dream of motherhood. Because infertility is so isolating, very few people knew what I was going through. I often wiped away tears before work and held them back until I returned home. Looking back, I recognize that was not the healthiest way to process my emotions, but I had never experienced anything like it before.

I brought my pain to God. My husband processed his emotions in his own way, and we struggled to support each other. After the second failed round of IUI, we decided to pause fertility treatments. I was not in the mental space to endure another disappointment. Instead, I focused on healing and continued to show up as a leader for my team.

The second circumstance that caused me to lament was the loss of my 17-year-old mini poodle, Mocha. She was gifted to me in college, and we quickly became inseparable. She was present for so many milestones in my life, from graduating from college to starting my first job and living on my own. She brought comfort during difficult times, especially when I was far from family. Losing her, especially so soon after my struggles with infertility, affected me deeply. I initially felt silly for grieving her loss, but the truth is that pets become family. After nearly two decades of memories, her absence was significant. There were days I laughed thinking about her and days I cried. In her final months, I could see her declining, but I prayed for more time. She was scheduled to be put down on a Monday, but a few days before, she passed away on her own terms. Letting her go was painful, but I continued forward, focusing on my responsibilities as a leader.

The third and most painful circumstance occurred in September 2023 when my grandmother passed away. Ruthella Johnson meant everything to me. She had a way of making you feel deeply loved and valued. She was an incredible woman of faith who consistently pointed me back to God. One of her favorite scriptures was Proverbs 3:5–6: "Trust in the Lord with all your heart and lean not on your own understanding; in all your ways acknowledge Him, and He shall direct your paths." She shared this verse so often that I now refer to it as "Ruthella's song."

In her final weeks, I was able to spend time with her. Even as her body weakened, her faith remained strong. I watched her lift her hands and praise God, even from her deathbed, and that is something I will never forget.

The last time I saw her, I knew it would be goodbye. I hugged and kissed her tightly, and she whispered, "I love you." I told her the same. Within hours of my flight landing, I received the call that she had passed away.

The grief that followed was overwhelming. I missed our daily conversations, our laughter, and her guidance. However, I found comfort in knowing she was with the Lord.

Although I never questioned God's plan, I still wished she could have stayed longer. In my grief, I asked God to comfort me, and He did. He surrounded me with support, even from a distance. Looking back, I wish I had allowed myself more time to process my grief instead of rushing back into work. I should have extended more grace to myself during that time.

The final circumstance that caused me to lament was marital separation. Out of respect for my husband, I will not share all the details, but after nearly eight years of marriage, we decided to separate. This came shortly after my grandmother's passing, adding another layer to my grief. This season drew me closer to God than ever before. My prayer life deepened as I sought understanding and strength. I had many questions, especially why I was facing so much at once. There were moments I felt like I could not continue, but God sustained me. In addition to prayer, I sought counseling to begin healing the broken areas of my heart. Over time, I began to recover spiritually, emotionally, and mentally. Through it all, I continued to lead. That responsibility never paused.

I share these experiences in hopes that they will help someone else. Although the past few years have been filled with challenges, they have also shaped me.

Every moment of grief has contributed to my purpose. Through it all, I have grown as an intercessor and deepened my relationship with God.

In April 2025, I founded a nonprofit in honor of my grandmother called Ruthella's Touch. Its mission is to empower individuals experiencing homelessness by providing spiritual nourishment, recreation, and resources that restore dignity, build self-esteem, and foster well-being for a brighter future. This organization is deeply personal to me, and I find great joy in serving others through it.

Out of the ashes of grief, God has revealed new dimensions of my purpose. He has not wasted any part of my story. I have emerged stronger, more focused, and more committed than ever before. Leadership is not always easy, but we must remember that God comforts us in our suffering. Lamenting allows us to express our pain while drawing closer to Him. With God and perseverance, every challenge can be overcome. Every obstacle is preparing you for your purpose, even when it comes at a cost.

About The Author

Dr. Rachel A. Watkins

Dr. Rachel A. Watkins is a pharmacy leader, intercessor, and compassionate community advocate. She is the founder of Ruthella's Touch, a nonprofit dedicated to empowering individuals experiencing homelessness through spiritual support and essential resources. Through her leadership and mentorship, she is committed to developing others and making a lasting impact in her community.

CHAPTER 6: SICK AND TIRED OF BEING SICK AND TIRED

Chela Whitehead

There comes a moment in life when you realize you are no longer just tired, but you are tired of being tired. Tired of carrying heartbreak.

Tired of feeling like you don't matter. Tired of silently wrestling with the feeling that you have been abandoned while still trying to show up like everything is fine and that was the place I found myself in.

From the outside, my life probably looked like I was holding it together. I was a mother, I worked, and I handled my responsibilities. But inwardly, I was exhausted in a way that sleep could not fix. I was surviving, but I was not truly living.

What weighed on me the most was not just what I had gone through, but what I feared. As a single mother, I carried the quiet burden of wondering if I was enough for my children. I questioned whether I was raising them the right way.

I worried about my son growing up without a man consistently in his everyday life, and I feared my daughters would one day face some of the same pain I had known. The thought that they might grow up feeling the same loneliness or questioning their worth the way I once had weighed heavily on me. I wanted something different for them, but at times I wondered if I was strong enough to break the cycle. Beneath my smile was a loneliness I rarely admitted out loud. I felt unseen, like nobody really knew how much I was carrying.

For a long time, I convinced myself that being strong meant handling everything on my own. I kept going, kept showing up for everyone else, even when I was running on empty. But strength without healing will eventually wear you down. And eventually, I reached a place where I could no longer ignore the weight I had been carrying inside. I didn't realize it then, but God was already preparing me for a moment that would change everything. The turning point came on a day I will never forget.

I remember going to church that day feeling completely worn down. I had been praying about the same situations over and over again, crying the same tears and asking God the same questions.

I was tired of the depression. Tired of feeling emotionally drained. Tired of trying to hold everything together. And that day, for the first time in a long time, I knew I couldn't carry it alone anymore.

One day, there came an opportunity for people to move forward with an altar prayer. Something inside of me told me to go. Normally, I would stay in my seat and pray quietly. But that day felt different. I was tired enough to move. I was tired enough to desperately stretch my way to the unknown. When I walked to the front, the pastor's mother began praying over me. We had barely spoken before, and she didn't know my story or the battles I had been fighting internally. But during that prayer, she spoke a scripture over my life that would stay with me forever. She prayed the words from Isaiah 40:31: "But those who wait upon the Lord shall renew their strength. They shall mount up with wings like eagles; they shall run and not grow weary; they shall walk and not faint."

When she spoke those words, something inside of me shifted. In that moment, I felt seen. I remember thinking, "How was it possible for her to see something in me when she barely knew me?" But it felt like God was speaking directly to the broken places in my heart.

That scripture became an anchor for me. Whenever I felt overwhelmed or questioned whether I was strong enough to keep going, those words reminded me that my strength didn't have to come from me; it came from God. For a long time, I even made it my phone's lock screen so that every time I looked at my phone, I would see the reminder: God was renewing my strength. Although the prayer didn't magically remove every struggle I was facing, it did give me something powerful: it gave me hope. For the first time in a long time, I believed that the weight I had been carrying would not be the end of my story.

After that day at church, something inside of me began shifting in ways I couldn't fully explain at the time. The situations in my life didn't immediately change, but my perspective slowly did. Instead of waking up each day already feeling defeated by what I was facing, I began to notice small moments where my heart felt lighter. The problems were still there. The responsibilities hadn't disappeared.

But something in me was no longer carrying the same weight. The scripture that had been spoken over me kept replaying in my mind, reminding me that God had not forgotten about me and that He was renewing my strength even when I didn't feel strong. So, instead of constantly asking, "Why is this happening to me?"

I slowly began asking a different question: "God, what are You trying to show me through this season?" That quiet shift in my thinking didn't solve everything overnight, but it planted something new in my heart, a growing sense that maybe this difficult season wasn't the end of my story.

For so long, I had been praying for God to remove the problems in my life. But during that season, I began to realize that sometimes God doesn't immediately remove the storm. Sometimes He strengthens you so that you can walk through it. That realization changed the way I approached my prayers. Instead of only asking God to fix everything around me, I began asking Him to work within me. I asked Him to help me heal, to help me understand the lessons hidden inside the pain, and to make me stronger through the process. Slowly, I began to notice changes in myself. I became more aware of my thoughts and started recognizing patterns in my life that I had ignored before.

There were moments when I had to face uncomfortable truths about myself, truths about how I responded to situations, the boundaries I had failed to set, and the ways fear and pain had influenced my decisions. Healing required honesty. And honesty meant I could no longer pretend that everything was fine when it wasn't.

The more honest I became with myself and with God, the more freedom I began to feel. It was as if layers of emotional weight were slowly being lifted from my shoulders. I realized that healing wasn't about pretending the past didn't hurt. It was about allowing God to restore the parts of me that had been wounded along the way.

From that moment forward, I began taking my healing more seriously. I started spending intentional time with God. Sometimes it was only a few quiet minutes in the morning. Other times it was simply sitting with Him while a worship song played softly in my mind before the day began. What started as a small change in my routine eventually became a daily habit. Monday through Sunday, I made it a point to acknowledge God first. However, before long, I noticed something interesting. On the days when I skipped that time with God, I could feel the difference. Something in my day felt off.

I felt less grounded and less peaceful. That's when I realized how important those moments had become. The more time I spent with God, the more clearly I began to recognize His voice in my life. What some people might call coincidences, I started recognizing as God moments, moments where His guidance and presence were undeniable.

During that season, journaling became one of the most powerful tools in my healing process. When I felt overwhelmed, I would write. I would pour my thoughts onto the page without judgment, allowing myself to be completely honest about what I was feeling. Sometimes the pages held my prayers. Other times, they held my tears, fears, frustrations, and questions for God. Writing gave me a safe place to release the emotions I had been carrying for so long, things I didn't always know how to say out loud. As I continued journaling, I began to notice something surprising. The more I wrote, the more clearly I could see the patterns in my thoughts and the ways God had quietly been guiding me all along. What started as a place to release my pain slowly became a place where I could also see God's faithfulness. One day, while journaling, a thought came to me: What if this could help someone else, too? What if the things I was learning in this season could encourage another woman who felt the same weight I had been carrying?

The more I thought about it, the more I realized that the process God was walking me through might not have been meant only for me. The prayers, the reflections, the honesty in those journal pages had helped me begin to see things differently. What started as a personal place of healing was slowly becoming something that could guide someone else through their own difficult season.

I began imagining what it would look like if other women had a place to pause, reflect, and process their own experiences with God the way I had been doing. A place where they could be honest about their struggles, their questions, and their hopes for healing.

That idea eventually grew into a 21-day guided healing journal designed to help others walk through their own season of reflection, faith, and personal growth. The name carries multiple meanings for me. On one level, it represents overcoming difficult seasons and choosing healing instead of remaining stuck in pain. But on a deeper level, ACE also represents the initials of my three children: Aubree, Cody, and Eliana. My children are my "why." They are the reason I continue pushing forward. They inspire me to work hard, pursue education, and strive to become the best version of myself.

As my healing journey continued, another area of my life began challenging me to grow even more as a mother. Being a mother is one of the greatest blessings in my life, but it is also one of the most challenging responsibilities I carry. As a single mother, there were many moments when the weight of providing, nurturing, and guiding my children felt overwhelming. I loved them deeply and wanted to give them everything they needed, yet there were times when I felt like I was constantly pouring from a place that was already running low. There were days when I felt like I was giving so much of myself to everyone around me that I had very little left for myself. I remember realizing something that was difficult to admit: while I was trying to be strong for everyone else, I was quietly becoming emotionally drained. I was giving so much emotional support and patience to other children at work that sometimes I came home with little energy left for my own children.

That realization hurt because my children deserve the very best version of me. That moment forced me to be honest with myself. If I wanted to create a healthier environment for my children, I had to continue doing the work within myself first. That realization eventually inspired the idea for Little Kid Big Emotions, a children's book designed to help kids understand and express their feelings.

I even used a picture of my daughter and me as inspiration for the characters in the story, turning something personal into a tool that could help other families connect with their children emotionally.

Around the same time, I began collecting reflections about the moments when I clearly felt God guiding my life. At first, these were simply personal notes I wrote for myself, little reminders of prayers that had been answered, unexpected encouragement that came at just the right time, or quiet moments when I sensed God gently redirecting my thoughts.

As I began writing these moments down, I started noticing something I had not fully recognized before: God had been present in my life in more ways than I realized. Even in seasons that felt confusing or painful, there were small signs of His guidance, His protection, and His faithfulness.

At first, these reflections were simply personal notes I wrote for myself. But over time, those reflections grew into something more meaningful, what I now call Divine Devotions reminders of the many ways God shows up in our lives when we are willing to slow down, pay attention, and listen. Looking back, it amazes me how all of these ideas were born from something simple: spending time with God, listening to His voice, and being obedient when He nudged me to act.

If there is one message I would want every woman reading my story to remember, it is this: fill your cup first. As women, we often serve as the foundation for our families. We hold things together, support others, and carry responsibilities that many people never see. But we cannot pour from an empty cup. Taking time to care for your emotional, spiritual, and mental well-being is not selfish; it is necessary. When we begin filling our own cups, we gain clarity about our boundaries, our purpose, and the environments we allow ourselves to remain in.

Another important lesson I learned is that real change begins within us. It's easy to offer advice to others or see clearly what someone else should do, but true transformation happens when we begin applying those same lessons to our own lives. Healing requires honesty, the kind of honesty that asks you to look inward and acknowledge the places that still need God's touch.

Above all, I have learned the importance of building a real relationship with God. Not a perfect one, but a consistent one. A relationship where you show up honestly, even when you don't have all the answers. Like any relationship, it requires communication, trust, and time.

The more I spent time with God, the more I began to understand that healing is not something that happens overnight. It unfolds over time as we allow Him to work within us. And that process often looks very different from what we expect. When people talk about the promised land, they often forget to talk about the process it takes to get there. We celebrate the destination but rarely acknowledge the journey that comes before it. Healing isn't always comfortable. Growth requires honesty, patience, and the willingness to face parts of ourselves we may have ignored for years. But it is in that process that transformation truly happens.

Looking back now, I can see that the broken pieces of my story were never wasted. The moments that once felt painful, confusing, or unfair were quietly shaping me into the woman I was becoming. God was using every experience, even the ones I didn't understand at the time, to prepare me for something greater. What once felt like the end of my strength was actually the beginning of my purpose.

About the Author

Chela Whitehead

Chela Whitehead is a writer, mother of three, and creative entrepreneur passionate about helping women heal and grow through faith and reflection. Through her work, including the Ace'd That Season Guided Journal, she encourages women to process life's challenges, rediscover their strength, and build healthier foundations for the future.

Meet the Authors

Kayana Lang

Kayana Lang was born in Heidelberg, Germany, on February 14, 1981. She is a devoted mother of four, carrying both the joy of motherhood and the pain of losing a child. Kayana is a nurse who is passionate about educating others on safe sexual practices and empowering individuals with knowledge about their health and available options. She is also the owner of "Yana's Beauty Treats," a business inspired by her personal battle with eczema, where her mission is reflected in her slogan, "Where Passion Meets Your Purpose."

As she continues to grow closer to God, Kayana is committed to sharing her life journey with transparency and faith. She believes her experiences are not just for her, but to encourage and uplift others. Through her testimony, she hopes to inspire healing, growth, and connection, gaining not only impact but also new sisters in Christ along the way.

E. N. McMillan

E. N. McMillan is a native of Augusta, GA, and the owner of More Than Ragz online boutique, where she manages six e-commerce sites. She is a contributor to The Brown Girl Guidebooks: Start with Self Love book and journal. She is a self-love advocate for women and was named the 2023 Amaro Literacy Mission – South Africa Leader of the Year. E. N. is committed to helping women own their pieces and move toward their purpose.

Debra S. Parker

Debra S. Parker is an author, registered nurse, and woman of unwavering faith whose life reflects resilience, healing, and purpose. She is the author of Finish This for Me: His Story, a Seventeen-Year-Old's Journey of Mustard Seed Faith, a powerful testament to trusting God even in life's most difficult moments. As a mother, grandmother, and great-grandmother, Debra carries generations of wisdom shaped by both love and hardship. After enduring years of traumatic experiences, she turned her pain into purpose through writing. Her voice is rooted in faith, transparency, and a deep desire to help others find hope. Through her work, Debra reminds readers that even the smallest seed of faith can produce powerful transformation.

Ashley Titus

Ashley Titus is a devoted wife, mother, and youth advocate committed to empowering the next generation.

As the Founder of A.S.H. Consultants, she leads a thriving mentorship and coaching organization that supports young people through life's challenges. Guided by her Christian faith, Ashley brings compassion, understanding, and purpose to her work with youth and families. She partners with schools, organizations, and communities to create safe spaces where young people can grow in confidence, resilience, and self-awareness. Through workshops, programs, and hands-on mentorship, she equips youth with leadership skills and emotional tools for success.

Ashley's belief in strong family dynamics strengthens her ability to connect with both parents and children. A visionary leader, she is dedicated to helping youth recognize their worth and step boldly into their future.

Dr. Rachel A. Watkins

Dr. Rachel A. Watkins is a dedicated pharmacy leader, intercessor, and compassionate community advocate. An Indianapolis native, she earned her Doctor of Pharmacy degree from Purdue University in 2008 before beginning her career in Charlotte, North Carolina. Over the past 17 years, she has served in a variety of hospital pharmacy roles, advancing through both clinical and leadership positions. In July 2025, she returned to Indianapolis, where she currently serves as a hospital pharmacy operations manager. Known for her heart for people, Dr. Watkins is passionate about mentorship and is committed to developing the next generation of pharmacy leaders and technicians. She finds joy in sharing her knowledge, encouraging others, and watching them reach their professional goals. In 2025, she founded Ruthella's Touch, a nonprofit organization created in honor of her late grandmother, Ruthella, who passed away in September 2023. The organization's mission is to empower individuals experiencing homelessness by providing spiritual nourishment, recreation, and essential resources that restore dignity, build self-esteem, and foster well-being.

Raised in a close-knit family grounded in faith and perseverance, Dr. Watkins is the youngest daughter of six children. Outside of her professional and nonprofit work, she enjoys community outreach, traveling, cooking, and spending meaningful time with friends and family.

Chela Whitehead

Chela Whitehead is a purpose-driven author, creative, and advocate for healing and growth. Originally from Michigan and now residing in Texas, she uses her voice and life experiences to inspire others to navigate life's most challenging seasons with faith and resilience. As the founder of Ace Divine Legacy, Chela creates impactful resources, including guided journals, devotionals, and children's books that promote emotional awareness and personal transformation. Her work is deeply rooted in authenticity, spirituality, and the belief that healing is a journey worth honoring. Through her writing, she encourages women and families to embrace their becoming and find strength in their stories.

Chela is also a dedicated mother and mentor, committed to uplifting the next generation through intentional connection and guidance. This anthology marks another step in her mission to turn pain into purpose and help others do the same.

LaTonya M. Whitehead

LaTonya M. Whitehead is an author, speaker, and purpose coach committed to helping women heal, grow, and walk boldly in their God-given purpose. As the visionary and founder of Empowered Women United, she has created a powerful community where women are equipped through transparency, biblical truth, and real-life application.

Through her own journey of overcoming brokenness, rejection, and life's hardest moments, LaTonya has become known for her raw storytelling and transformative teaching style that meets women right where they are. She is the author of I Got Issues: Finding Purpose After Your Pieces and the creator of the From Pieces to Purpose™ movement.

This anthology reflects her heart to create a space where real women can share real stories and experience real transformation. LaTonya continues to use her voice to empower others to turn their pain into purpose and their stories into impact.

About Empowered Women United™

Empowered Women United is more than a name. It is a movement. A movement of women who are choosing to heal, grow, and walk boldly in their purpose.
This is a space where broken pieces are not hidden, they are acknowledged, healed, and transformed.

Where real women have real conversations and expect real results.

We meet weekly to encourage one another, grow in faith, and hold each other accountable to becoming who God has called us to be.

This is not about perfection. This is about progress.

And whether you are just beginning your journey or learning how to rebuild.

There is a place for you here.

A Final Word

If you've made it this far, you didn't just read a book—you witnessed courage.

Every story you've encountered in these pages is more than a moment. It is proof that pain does not have the final say. That broken pieces can still build something beautiful. That perseverance is not just something we talk about—it is something we live. These women chose to open their hearts, not because it was easy, but because someone else needed to know they are not alone.

And now that someone is you.

Maybe you saw yourself in these pages. Maybe you felt something shift.

Maybe you realized that your story isn't over, it's just been waiting for you to give it a voice. This is your reminder:

You are not disqualified by what you've been through.

You are not too broken, too late, or too far gone. There is purpose in you right now, as you are.

Empowered Women United is more than a name. It is a call.

A call to heal. A call to grow. A call to rise.

A call to use your voice, even if it shakes.

We are building a community of women who are done hiding, done shrinking, and done believing the lie that their past defines them.

If these stories stirred something in you, don't

ignore it. Lean into it.

Grow through it.

And when you're ready…

Join us.

There is a place for you here.

9 798995 502401